What Are Feelings?

by Isabel Thomas

illustrated by Shahab Shamshirsaz

What Are Feelings?

Have you ever giggled so hard,
you could not talk?

Have you ever been frightened? Your belly can turn to jelly! If you are angry, your whole body can tremble.

Feelings can be very strong. They can affect your whole body.

What are feelings for? How do they get inside you? Let's **investigate**.

Brain Power

Feelings happen in your **brain**.

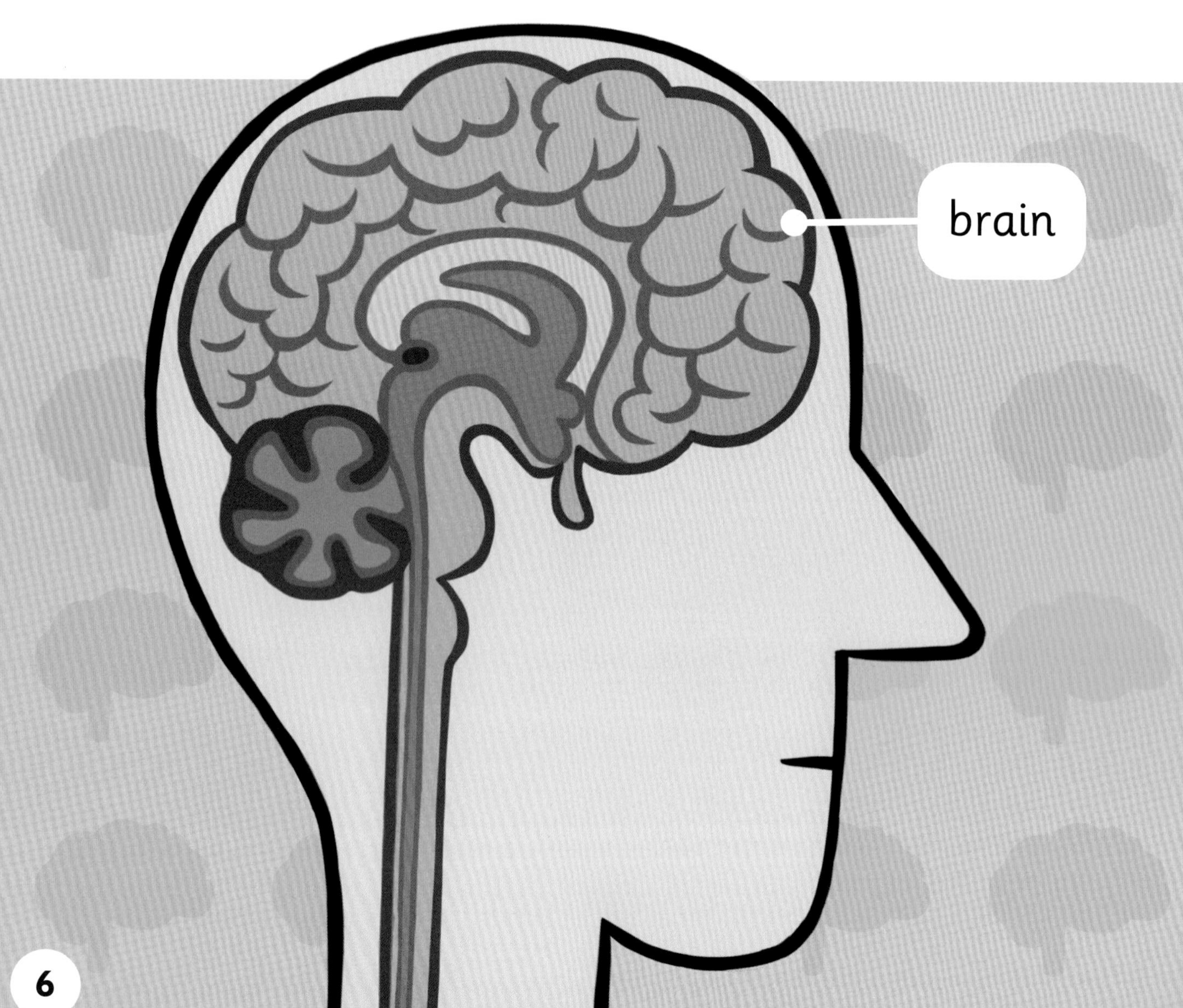

When your body **senses** something, your brain thinks. Then your brain tells your body what to do.

When you think, your brain must do these things.

1. Your brain checks your **memory**.
2. Your brain **predicts** what might happen next.

3. Your brain plans different things you could do.
4. Your brain selects the best one.

Feelings also happen when your body senses something.

However, feeling is different from thinking. Feelings appear faster. They help you act faster, too.

How Can Feelings Help?

When you are high up, you might feel frightened.

Feeling frightened can stop you if something seems unsafe.

Feelings help us act quickly.

Different People, Different Feelings

Different people can have different feelings. Even about the same thing!

All the things you have seen and done shape your feelings.

Your brain can use a memory to help make a feeling.

Show this to different people. Who feels frightened? Who feels fine?

Remember some people may have different feelings about the same thing.

How to Cope with Feelings

It is normal to have lots of feelings.

Some feelings can be very strong.

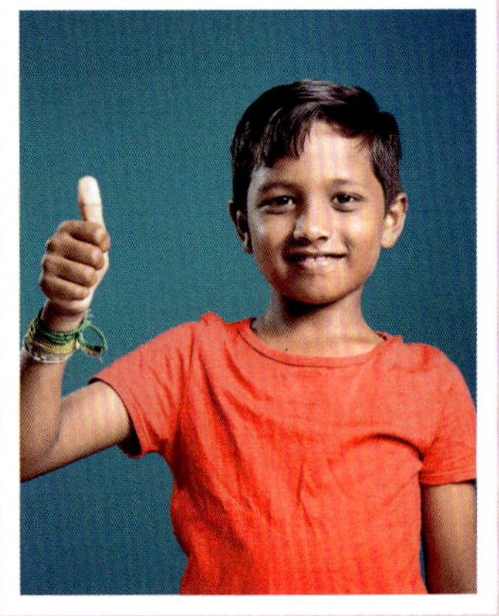

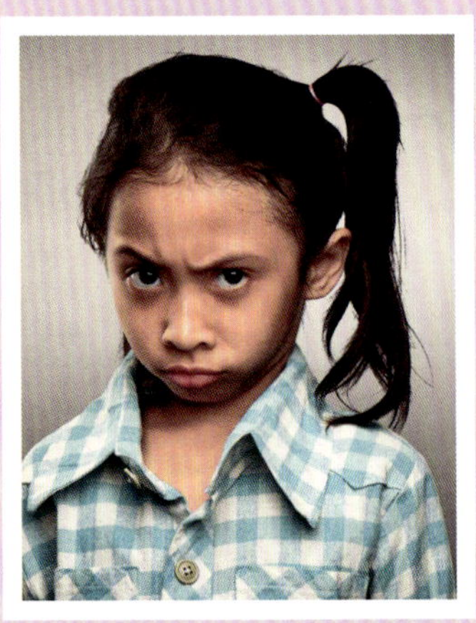

The thinking part of your brain can help.
It helps you to cope with feelings.

You might feel angry, sad or frightened. It is good to think about what brings about these feelings.

See if these things help.

Go for a walk.

Take air in and push it out.

Talk about your feelings.

Look It Up

brain: the part inside your skull that controls what happens in your body

investigate: look closely

memory: something from the past that you can still think about

predict: to think what might happen next

senses: detects something using sight, smell, taste, sound or skin contact

Index